Calico Critters™

Calico Critters™

COUNTRY SCHOOL
Calico Critters™

Calico Critters™

Calico Critters™

Hot dogs
Calico Critters™

Calico Critters™

BAKERY
FRESH & ORGANIC
SUPER MARKET

ERMARKET

Calico Critters™

Sylvanian Families®

Calico Critters™

ORIGINAL
Sylvanian families®

Made in the USA
Coppell, TX
06 September 2024

36912335R00031

Happy
Birthday
Sylvanian Families®